YUMMY SALAD RECIPES

Palatable Salad Recipes

Filled With Awesomeness

By

Jane Philips

Appreciation

It is a great honor to provide awesome salad recipes for you. I am delighted to be of service, and I hope this cookbook is of great help.

In a special way, I also want to use this opportunity to thank all those that helped me in one way or the other, directly or indirectly, in making this book a success. Much love!

Baja Chicken Pasta Salad

Ingredients to use

- 1/4 teaspoon Salt
- 3/4 pound Chicken Breast -- *
- 2 tablespoons Sour Cream Or Plain Yogurt
- 1/2 cup Mayonnaise Or Salad Dressing
- 1 cup Ring Macaroni Or Orzo -- Raw
- 1 teaspoon Red Chiles – Ground
- 6 ounces Dried Mixed Fruit -- **
- 1 cup Jicama – Cubed
- 2 Green Onions/Tops -- Sliced

NOTE: * The chicken breast should be boneless, skinless and weigh about

3/4

*** You should use 1 6-oz package of diced mixed fruit.*

How to prepare

1. In a 4 quart Dutch oven, heat salted water, just enough to immerse the chicken breast (about ¼ tsp to a cup of water).
2. Now, put the chicken breast into it, cover it, and allow it to heat till it gets boiling.
3. Reduce the heat and simmer until the chicken gets done, which should take about fifteen (15) to twenty (20) minutes.
4. Using a slotted spoon, remove the chicken.
5. Heat water to a boil, then, in a gradual manner, add fruit and ring macaroni or orzo as the water keeps boiling.
6. Boil uncovered, stirring from time to time, about six (6) to eight (8) minutes until the ring macaroni becomes soft, then drain. If you are using the orzo, then allow it to boil for about ten (10) minutes, then drain.

7. Use cold water and rinse, then drain again.
8. Now, slice the chicken into pieces about ½ inches, then combine and mix together with the macaroni, fruit, onions and jicama.
9. The remaining ingredients should be mixed and tossed together with the chicken mixture.
10.   Finally, cover it, then transfer into the fridge, allowing it to chill for at least two (2) hours.
11.   Enjoy!

Adreana's Greek Pasta Salad

Ingredients you will need:

- 3 stalks celery -- chopped
- 1 pound rotini
- 3 green onions -- finely sliced
- 1 red bell pepper – chopped
- 16 ounces Italian salad dressing
- 2 1/4 ounces black olives – sliced
- 1 pound boneless skinless chicken breasts
- 4 ounces feta cheese -- drained & crumbled

How to prepare:

1. Have the chicken cooked in water to cover with one (1) bay leaf.
2. Bring it to boil, then cook until the juices run clear, for about thirty (30) minutes.

3. Let it cool, then peel off the skins.
4. Alternatively, you can use a frying pan to cook the chicken until it gets cooked through.
5. Slice into tiny bits.
6. Have the noodles cooked, then drain.
7. Add all ingredients, then mix properly.
8. You may use only just half of the salad dressing bottle, then keep the rest on the table in case someone wants some more.
9. Finally, serve warm or cold, enjoy!

Basic Potato Salad

Ingredients you will need

- 3 tablespoons vinegar
- 2 pounds new potatoes
- pepper
- 1/2 pound mushrooms
- 3 stalks celery
- 3 green onions
- 2 hard-boiled eggs
- 1/4 cup mayonnaise
- 2 tablespoons Dijon mustard
- Salt

How to prepare

1. Get a pan, place the potatoes in it, then cover it with water, place over high heat, and allow it to boil.
2. Cook until the potatoes become soft.

3. Now, slice the mushrooms, celery and onions thinly, then combine together in a mixing bowl.
4. When the potatoes get soft, drain, then halve or quarter them, depending on the sizes, then transfer into bowl.
5. Use vinegar and sprinkle, cover it, then transfer to the fridge to chill.
6. When it gets chilled, slice the eggs, then add to bowl.
7. Now, add the mustard and the mayonnaise, then to taste, use salt and pepper to season it, mixing all together in a gentle manner.
8. Enjoy!

Aegean Artichoke & Penne Pasta Salad

Ingredients to use

- 1/2 pound penne pasta
- 1/4 cup lemon juice
- 2 cloves garlic -- minced
- 2 tablespoons olive oil
- 6 fresh baby artichokes
- 3 tablespoons fresh basil -- or 1 tsp. dried
- Juice of one lemon
- 1/2 teaspoon salt
- 2 tablespoons capers
- 1/4 teaspoon black pepper
- 3 tablespoons fresh parsley
- 1/2 cup olives – Kalamata
- 1/2 cup fresh tomato -- chopped
- 1/2 cup feta cheese – optional
- 1/2 cup tomato juice

How To Prepare

1. Slice off the stems from the artichokes, and peel the tough outer layers off, so that the yellow green hearts will become visible.
2. After that, slice the artichokes into quarters, then get a medium bowl and mix together ¼ cup of the lemon juice with two (2) cups of water.
3. In order to prevent discoloration, transfer the artichokes to the lemon water, then toss.
4. drain it, steam the artichokes for about twenty (20) minutes until it becomes tender, then chill.
5. Get a large pot, then pour two (2) quarts of water into it, and allow it to boil rapidly.
6. Now add one (1) teaspoon of salt and penne.
7. Cook the penne until it gets soft, for about ten (10) minutes.
8. Drain it, then use cold water to rinse.
9. To prepare salad dressing, mix and combine together in a blender or food processor the olive

oil, tomato juice, pepper, lemon juice, basil, parsley, garlic, and salt, then puree for thirty (30) seconds.

10.   In a large salad bowl, toss and combine properly the penne, capers, artichokes, feta cheese and olives.

11.   Pour in the dressing, toss well and finally, enjoy!

Apricot Salad

Ingredients you will need:

For the first step

- 1 large jar apricot baby food (8-10 oz)
- 2 small or 1 large box of apricot jello
- 1 can crushed pineapple -- (16 oz) drained
- (retain juice!)

For the second step

- 1 pkg dreamwhip (1 envelope)
- 1 pkg cream cheese -- (8 oz)

For the third step

- 1 egg
- 1 Tbsp flour (heaping)

- 1 c pineapple juice (add water to juice
- retained to make a full cup)
- 1 Tbsp butter
- 3/4 c sugar

How to prepare

First step:

using just 3½ cups water, mix the jello.

Now, add the baby food and the pineapple too, then transfer into a pan with size 11x14 inch, allowing it to chill until it gets firm.

Second step:

Prepare the cream whip as specified.

Beat in the cream cheese, spread on jello, then chill, until it gets thick.

Third step:

Combine the ingredients for this third step and cook until it gets thick.

Allow to cool.

Spread on top, then chill.

Bavarian Potato Salad

Ingredients to use

- 2 tablespoons Lemon juice
- 4 cups Potatoes -- *
- 1/3 cup Onion – chopped
- 2 cups Chicken broth -- **
- 1/2 teaspoon Sugar
- 1/2 teaspoon Salt
- Pepper -- as desired
- 1/4 cup Vegetable oil

Note: *Potatoes should be peeled and sliced 1/4-inch thick.*

 *** Chicken broth may be either homemade or commercial.*

How to prepare:

1. For about five (5) to eight (8) minutes, using ¼ salt, have the potatoes boiled in broth until it gets tender. Then drain
2. With vegetable oil and onions, toss the warm potatoes.
3. In lemon juice, have the ¼ of the remain salt dissolved.
4. Now, pour it over the potatoes.
5. Finally, have the salad marinated before serving, for about one (1) to two (2) hours.
6. Ensure you serve at room temperature.
7. Enjoy!

Antipasto Salad

Ingredients to use:

- 1/2 cup grated Parmesan cheese
- 4 ounces provolone cheese, cut into -- 2 x 1/4" strips
- 6 ounce can pitted ripe olives -- drained/sliced
- 6 oz. jar marinated artichoke hearts -- drained/chopped
- 9 oz. package frozen spinach, thawed -- squeezed to drain
- 1 1/2 cups prepared creamy Italian salad dressing
- 4 ounces chopped salami
- 1 teaspoon Dijon mustard
- 16 oz. pkg fresh/frozen cheese tortellini
- 2 ounce jar diced pimiento, drained -- if desired
- 11 oz. can corn -- drained

How to prepare:

1. Cook the tortellini to the doneness you want, just as it is specified on the package.
2. Have it drained, then rinse with cold water.
3. Get a very large bowl, then combine together the salami, tortellini, corn, provolone cheese, 1 cup of the olives, artichoke hearts and spinach.
4. This time, get a small bowl and combine the salad dressing, the mustard, and also ¼ cup of the parmesan cheese, then mix together properly, until well incorporated.
5. Spread the dressing over the salad, and mix in a gentle manner.
6. Have it covered, then place in the fridge to chill for about one (1) to two (2) hours so that the flavors get incorporated.

7. If desired, just before you serve, garnish it with pimiento.
8. Enjoy!

Autumn Jewels Gelatin Salad

Ingredients to use:

- 6 ounces red gelatin
- 2 apples
- 2 cups boiling water
- 15 ounces crushed pineapple
- 1/2 cup sugar
- 1 cup celery – diced
- 1 cup cranberries
- 1/2 cup nuts -- chopped

*NOTE: * Use pecans, walnuts, or a mixture of both.*

How to prepare:

1. Into very little pieces, slice the apples, cranberries and celery.
2. Have the pineapple drained, then keep the juice separate.
3. Mix together cranberries, sugar and apple, cover it, then keep in the fridge while making the remaining salad.
4. With boiling water, mix together gelatin, then stir until it gets melted.
5. Add plenty of water or fruit juice (strawberry nectar, apricot nectar, etc.) to the pineapple juice so that it adds up to one (1) cup.
6. Now, pour this into the gelatin mixture, then transfer into the refrigerator for it to chill, until it begins to get thick.
7. Mix together the cranberry-apple mixture with the drained pineapple, celery and also nuts.
8. Gently stir this into the gelatin mixture.

9. After that, transfer into molds that are lightly greased or into individual serving molds, then move into the fridge to chill until it gets solid.

10. When firm, unmold, then serve on a platter of lettuce, or you can garnish with sour cream, or even with whipped cream that has been sweetened, and also sprinkle lightly with a pinch of cinnamon.

Note: You can serve this with your thanksgiving meal.

Bean and Tuna Salad

Ingredients to use:

- 2 cans Cannellini beans
- 1 teaspoon Salt
- 1/3 cup Olive oil
- Fresh pepper to taste
- 3 teaspoons Red wine vinegar
- 12 ounces Tuna – drained
- 1 medium Red onion
- 3 cups Water

How to prepare:

1. Combine and mix together the vinegar, oil, pepper and salt.
2. Get a shallow bowl, then pour this mixture over beans and onions.

3. Have it covered, then refrigerate it for at least one (1) hour.
4. Using a slotted spoon, transfer the bean mixture onto a serving plate.
5. Finally, divide the tuna into tiny bits and spread around the bean mixture.

Bacon-Avocado Potato Salad

Ingredients to use

- 8 slices bacon
- 1 tablespoon fresh cilantro – chopped
- 2 avocados – cubed
- salt
- 1 tablespoon fresh lime juice
- paprika
- 1/2 cup white wine
- 1/2 cup chopped onions -- chopped
- 1/4 cup cider vinegar
- 6 medium boiling potatoes
- 1/4 teaspoon mustard powder
- black pepper
- 2 tablespoons fresh parsley -- chopped

How to prepare

1. With their skin still intact, boil the potatoes.
2. As the potatoes are boiling, cube the avocados, then toss, using lime juice.
3. Chop the bacon into an inch in size, then, in a large skillet, fry, until it gets crisp.
4. Take the bacons out, place on paper towels to drain.
5. Inside bacon fat, sauté onions until it gets golden
6. Take down the pan from heat, then, to taste, add in and stir salt, wine, mustard, vinegar, paprika and pepper.
7. When the potatoes get soft, drain, then peel, and dice them.
8. With the potatoes still warm, pour the dressing over them, then mix well.
9. Allow it to cool to room temperature, then fold in the avocado, the bacon, the parsley, and then the cilantro.

10. Finally, serve at room temperature, or, as an alternative, refrigerate for one (1) hour or longer.

11. Enjoy!

Autumn Fruit Salad

Ingredients to use

- 1 teaspoon cinnamon
- 1 sliced bananas
- 1/2 pound red grapes
- 1 Granny Smith apple
- 1 tablespoon apple cider
- 1/2 cup almond slivers -- toasted
- 2 red delicious apples
- 1/4 teaspoon ground ginger
- 2 Bartlett pears
- 1/2 teaspoon nutmeg
- 1 cup vanilla yogurt

How to prepare

1. Wash the apples and pears, then core them. You can peel them if you want.
2. Cut them into chunks, one (1) inch thick.
3. Get the bananas sliced to ½" thick.
4. Wash the grapes, then slice in half.
5. Get a salad bowl, and in it, mix and combine the almonds and fruits.
6. Mix the yoghurt with cider and spices, then spread over the fruit salad.
7. Ensure that you stir for an even coating of the fruits.
8. Finally, chill.
9. Enjoy!

24-Hour Slaw

Ingredients to use:

- 2 lg red onions -- thinly sliced
- 1 lg. head cabbage -- shredded/not chopped
- 3/4 cup sugar
- Hot Dressing – (recipe below)

How to prepare:

1. Pour the sugar into cabbage and stir.
2. In a very large bowl, place half of the cabbage.
3. Have it covered with slices of onions.
4. The next thing is to top it with the cabbage that is remaining.
5. Now, in a slow manner, pour the boiling hot dressing over. (recipe for the hot dressing below)
6. Do not stir.

7. Cover and immediately transfer to the fridge to chill.
8. Let it chill for twenty-four (24) hours.
9. After chilling, stir properly and serve!
10.   Enjoy!

To prepare the hot dressing:

You will need:

- 1 cup cider vinegar
- 1 1/2 teaspoons salt
- 1 teaspoon sugar
- 1 teaspoon celery seeds
- 1 cup oil
- 1 teaspoon dry mustard

How to prepare

1. In a saucepan, mix and combine together the sugar, celery seeds, salt, mustard and vinegar.
2. Let it arrive at a rolling boil.
3. Now, add oil, and stir as you do, then return it to a rolling boil.

Avocado with Groundnut Dressing

Ingredients to use

- 1 tablespoon lemon juice
- salt -- to taste
- 2 tablespoons peanuts -- shelled
- 2 avocados -- ripe
- 1/2 teaspoon cinnamon
- 1/2 teaspoon paprika
- fresh chives -- to garnish
- cayenne -- to taste

How to prepare

1. have the avocados peeled, cut the stone out, then slice into cubes.
2. Use lemon juice to sprinkle it, then keep separate.
3. Have the peanuts grounded roughly using a rolling pin, or, as an alternative, you can use a grinder.

4. Now, combine the peanuts and spices, then mix properly.
5. Spread the mixture over the avocados, together with finely chopped chives.
6. Finally, transfer into the fridge and let it chill, until it becomes ready to serve.
7. Enjoy!

Artichoke Salad

Ingredients to use:

- 1 Tablespoon Lemon juice
- 2 Cups Artichoke hearts, quartered
- 2 Teaspoons Salt
- Small garlic clove- 1 Each
- Fresh artichoke hearts- 4 Each
- 1 Teaspoon Lea & Perrins
- 1 Tablespoon Wine vinegar
- 3 Tablespoons Olive oil
- 1 Teaspoon Louisiana hot sauce

How to prepare

1. Get a wooden salad bowl, and inside it, use a strong fork to combine and mash garlic and salt.
2. Add the fresh artichoke hearts, then blend together with the salt and garlic.
3. Add olive oil and stir, then add lemon juice and stir too.

4. Add the wine vinegar and stir, add the hot sauce, stir, then add the Lea & Perrins Worcestershire sauce, stir and mix properly.
5. Transfer canned artichoke hearts in the dressing, then let it marinate for about one (1) hour.
6. After that, you can eat like that, or you can serve in on a platter of green beans.

Balsamic Dressing

Ingredients to use:

- 3 teaspoons Capers
- 3/4 cup Water
- 1 tablespoon Fresh parsley -- chopped (opt)
- 2 teaspoons Dijon mustard
- 1/4 cup Balsamic vinegar
- 1 1/2 teaspoons Dried basil

How to Prepare

1. Mix all the ingredients together
2. You should adjust vinegar to your desired taste as it has a strong flavor.
3. Store it inside a container in the refrigerator.

Apple and Fennel Salad

Ingredients to use

- 1 each Small Fennel Head -- sliced
- 5 ounces Fresh Spinach
- 1 each Small Red Onion -- sliced
- 2 each Medium Granny Smith Apples

How to prepare

1. Peel and cube the apples.
2. Wash the spinach thoroughly, ensuring that the fibrous stems are removed.
3. Dry it, then transfer into the salad bowl.
4. Now, add the fennel, onions and apples.
5. You should toss with celery seed dressing.
6. Finally, trim with fennel tops.

7. Enjoy!

Barbecue Cubes

Ingredients to use

- Pepper -- Dash Of
- 8 ounces Tomato Sauce -- (1 can)
- 3/4 cup -- Boiling Water
- 1 1/2 teaspoons Vinegar
- 3 ounces Lemon Jell-O -- (1 Pkg.)
- 1 tablespoon Horseradish
- 1/2 teaspoon Salt

How to prepare:

1. In water that is boiling, have the jell-0 dissolved
2. Combine and mxi together the other ingredients

3. When the Jell-O gets to room temperature, add the ingredients and mix well.
4. Transfer into an oiled 8-inches square pan.
5. Transfer into the refrigerator and chill until it becomes solid.
6. Slice into cubes, then serve on top of salad, which you will use for your barbecue.
7. Enjoy!

Another Bean Salad

Ingredients to use:

- 16 ounces Yellow beans, can -- drained
- 1/2 teaspoon Salt
- 4 each Celery – sliced
- 16 ounces Green beans, can – drained
- 1 each Green pepper -- slivered
- 16 ounces Lima beans, can – drained
- 1 cup Sugar
- 16 ounces Garbanzo beans, can -- drained
- 16 ounces Red kidney beans -- drained
- 3 each Onions, medium -- sliced thin
- 1 cup Vinegar

How to prepare:

1. In a pan, mix and combine together the salt, vinegar, sugar, then for one (1) minute, bring to boil. Let it cool.
2. Mix and toss together the other ingredients, then spread the other ingredients generously over them.
3. Let it marinate in the fridge for twenty four (24) hours, stirring occasionally.

Bavarian Sausage Salad

Ingredients to use

- 1/4 teaspoon Pepper
- 1/2 pound Knockwurst -- cooked / cooled
- 1/4 teaspoon Paprika
- 3 tablespoons Vinegar
- 1 tablespoon Capers
- 2 tablespoons Vegetable oil
- 1 each Onion -- medium
- 1/2 teaspoon Salt
- 2 each Pickles -- small
- 1/4 teaspoon Sugar
- 1 tablespoon Mustard -- prepared *
- 1 tablespoon Parsley – chopped

*NOTE: * the Mustard should be the Gulden Type or strong Djon.*

How to prepare

1. Into very small cubes, slice the knockwurst.
2. crumble the onion and pickles.
3. Combine and mix together the mustard, vinegar and oil.
4. Now, add pepper, salt, sugar and paprika too.
5. If you wish, you can adjust the seasonings.
6. Pour in the capers, and mix very properly.
7. Pour and stir in the thinly sliced knockwurst, onions and pickles.
8. Finally, just before you serve, adorn it with chopped parsley.

Apple Cider Salad

Ingredients to use

- 1/4 teaspoon salt
- 2 packages gelatin powder – unflavored
- 1/4 cup black walnuts -- chopped
- 2 cups apple cider
- lettuce leaves -- for decoration
- 1 tablespoon chopped parsley
- 2 cups apples -- diced
- cooking oil

How to prepare

1. into a small bowl, place cold water, about ½ cup.
2. Now, into the water, spray about two tablespoons of unflavored gelatin, then leave it for about five (5) to ten (10) minutes to get soft.

3. Have about two (2) cups of apple cider heated it gets really hot, then add salt to it,
4. Take it from the fire, then immediate add the gelatin that has been left to get soft.
5. Stir this until the gelatin gets totally melted.
6. Get a one (1) quart mold ready by greasing it lightly using cooking oil. Use cooking oil, not olive oil.
7. Now, using a spoon, transfer about ½ cup of the gelatin mixture into the mold, then put it in the refrigerator.
8. Chill the mixture remaining until it gets a bit thicker than the thickness of unbeaten white egg.
9. Just before the large bowl of gelatin gets to the desired consistency, have the apples diced, then chop parsley and walnuts.
10.   Now, have this to the gelatin then place it into the mold that is already having a thin bottom layer of gelatin.
11.   Chill, until it gets set.

12. Finally, unmold and move to a serving plate that has already gotten decorated with lettuce leaves. A great choice is curly endive.

Printed in Great Britain
by Amazon

41495615R00031